Acknowledgements

Regie Gibson would like to thank:
My children Jamila, Safiya, and Jordan, and my wife Kate, Lillie an[...] Gibson, Stephanie Miller and Angelina KurLweg, Brenda Lee Major, Kwodwo Karl Fletcher of Africa West Bookstore, Laurence Jones of Laurence Jones, Chuck Perkins, Nate Germany, Lasana Cazembe, Muhammad Akil, Sonya Pouncy, Philip Koenig, Nina Corwin, Michael Warr, the great and mighty Marc "slampappi so what" Smith, National Poetry Slam, Inc., Patricia Smith, Michael Brown, Theodore Witcher, Mama Maria McCray (first person to let me on the mic, she's been regretting it ever since), Reality and Sikeman keep reaching for the words, Debra "collage" Grison, Malik Yusef, Orron Kenyatta, William King, Cory from Eastwind Productions, Susana Sandoval, Kahil EL' Zubar, Ifa Bayeza, Mama Kemba, Teresa Wiltz, Achy Obejas, Tanya Bruggera, Kent Forman, Tyehimba Jess, David Miller, Kurt Vonnegut, Van and Cathy Baldwin, Donna Demiers, Liberty 0 Daniels, Kwodwo Otis Grant, Tony Crooks, the entire gang from Spices (you had to be there), Touch of the Past, the Green Mill, the old Lit-X crew, Mario, Tina and Kendall (oh my!), the Guild Complex, every venue, university, church mosque synagogue temple and kingdom hall which has allowed me to be a part of your energy.

extra special thanks:

Daniel Ferri, Ron Allen and Vivee Frances for your advice and guidance in my professional as well as personal life. If your love and wisdom has an end I haven't seen it.

Tara J. Betts for guidance and direction in the countless hours of corrections, proofing and editing. For the books and the worlds you have introduced me to and for expanding and deepening me.

EM Press would like to thank the following people for their help with the release of our first publication: Dr. Joann Maruszak, Emily Rose Maruszak, Michelle Mega, Greg Harms, Marc Smith, Jeff Helgeson, Dr. Dick Prince, Dr. George Miller, and, of course, Regie Gibson— a poet.

SECOND EDITION

"Gibson is a National Poetry Slam Champion, co-writer for the loosely autobiographical film love jones (1997), and a poet of resonant power on the page as well as the stage. In his first book, he calls his poems chants and canticles, and they are both rhythmic and songlike. He writes often of music, paying tribute to jazzmen and Jimi Hendrix and writing wryly that God is a "blooz man." Wordplay is a defining element in Gibson's exploration of the plexus of spoken and written language, and as the title suggests, Gibson looks within and writes concretely about the flickerings of feelings, thoughts, memories, and desire. His poems are weather reports of the soul, erotic reveries, and red-hot attempts at seduction. There's a beat aura here, a la Leroi Jones/Amiri Baraka, and a velvety strain of psychedelia. Gibson's poems can seem facile, but they're rich in archetypes and a cosmic sensibility, and when he does turn his gaze to the outer world, he writes with clarity, wit, and warmth."---By Donna Seaman

AMERICAN LIBRARY ASSOCIATION (ALA) BOOKLIST

EM Press, LLC.

709 Marion St. * Joliet, IL 60436
www.em-press.com

Cover design/image manipulation
Gregory Harms/FARMHOUSE/ga
www.farmhouse-ga.com

Storms Beneath the Skin

Contents

Coos

Chants

--bird in labor with trane and sanders
--hykoo - meelaz kissez
--dance jamila dance
--jazz people
--hykoo - punk ass
--hykoo - hint from da baka da bus
--hykoo - jookin

--brotha to the night
(suite)

--funknawledgy
--its a teenage thang
--hykoo - voodoo chile
--eulogy of jimi christ
--the word

Canticles and Curses
(love letters found on a vagabond muse)

eyes
mind
blood
breath
belief
pilgrim
thirst
obeisance

--blooz man

Coos

alchemy

PRONOUN / NOUN / PREPOSITION / NOUN
PRONOUN / NOUN / PREPOSITION / NOUN
PRONOUN / ADJECTIVE / VERB / NOUN / PREPOSITION / NOUN
NOUN / VERB / ADVERB / CONJUNCTION / ARTICLE /NOUN
PREPOSITION / PRONOUN / NOUN

this / eroticism / of / language
this / copulation / of / words
this / slow / burning / fuck / of / syllables
poetry / is / more / than / the / sum
of / its / parts

(written to a professor friend i was on a literary panel with
who gave a short presentation insisting that poetry is little more
than the mechanics of grammar)

prayer

for the drummers hands
severed before they could strike skin

for the seventh string of unplayed guitars
gone suicidal with longing

for the fifth tendon of the hobbled upright

the fourth key of discarded trumpets
tortured into silent confession

prayer for the ghostly grey keys of murdered pianos
condemned to inhabit the cadavers of their killers

prayer for every dancers legs
stolen and pawned

for all poets made to eat their tongues

the artists eyes painted shut by the color blind

the singers throat made mausoleum
of infant hymns

this elegy is for your aborted souls

your mahabarata suffocated while dreaming of birth

your music massacred while praying

your song assassinated in flight

for you whose flames
could have scorched

open paths between us
and ourselves

and for us
condemned to never know it

poet woman

*(for sonia sanchez audre lorde sonya pouncy
patricia smith and adrienne rich and all womyn
with the ovaries to speak truth)*

amazon of song

valkyrie riding astride
blue horses chanting
mysteries

killer of the killer
of your childrens dreams

poet woman

blueberry terror
wearing a halo of black riddles

blessed handful of manna
meandering toward mouth
of morning hunger

birthmark singing
in the azure hand of day

you are screaming godspell

soprano choir
setting fire
to skies of dried silences
slaughtered by the thunder
of your tongue:
a slender sliver wrapped
around the pulsating trigger
of a crossbow

propelling your voice
like arrow of holy water at my skull
you speak
and the living music

11

of spinning spheres
guide my feet
i close my eyes and
your words are
transparent fists
shattering darkness
into pieces of new meaning

biting into the pomegranate of your
mouth i taste the blood of mans resurrection

perigee

(an invocation to be read when moon is full
and closest to the earth
and may be modified as reader wishes)

o moon

whole note
played on thighs of dawn
rhythm of hyacinth threaded
through jasmine song

o moon

ochre eye of a black griffin
floating in the amniotic aquarium
of space

birth earthward
your cry
through pathways
of wind riff
rise to our polymythic prayers

o moon

nipple-less tit of an amazon

o moon

sweet round eye of divine translucence

sermon upon us a new bleeding
as we sit beneath the canopy of ourselves
singing the canticles of ourselves
casting our lots to the sky
and reading the bones of memory

sermon us the new vision
of our past lives
while we sit and search blue sand for footnotes
of our ancestors footprints
tonight we ask that you send us all demons
and teach us to speak
in forgotten tongues of ovum and semen
staining the glass windows of language

teach us to unhum passion
from the vein of human tragedy
and learn to love through the anguish of now

tonight we cast our shadows
of djali and egun phrases
of our blood red blues

cotton-myth our stories
around ritual fire
as our poets prophets and priests
kill the space between planets and atoms

tonight we gather to speak
the eulogy of years

to kiss the sigh which burns
inside the oneness of human tears

o love live   o moon give

let us celebrate
deaths death

celebrate births birth

let us take the string between
mother and baby
and bury it in the earth
let our loins dance

14

new dances
for old and new reasons
toward seasons sad
with exuberance

let our tongues
become humming drums of light

while we chant the sanskrit
and blood language of coming sunrises

o moon

Perigee:

The point in the orbit of a satellite when it comes closest to the earth. It was the second night of a full moon cycle in March of 1997 when a friend and I attended a concert at the Hot House in Chicago. We came to check out an all female jazz ensemble. The leader of the band remarked to the crowd that they had spent so much time together writing music in preparation for this night, that their periods had synchronized.

My friend had told me earlier that she had gotten her "moon" as well. Growing up in a home with only one woman in the house, I had no idea that women could have synchronized periods. This was a revelation of grand proportion. This poem came to me that night at the Hot House while the ensemble played a composition called "The Peroid Suite: Music Written in Blood."

whisper

whisper me daggers and moonbeams
of loves convulsing paroxysms

whisper names of future lovers
their nightmare eyes obliterating language

whisper like daybreak dancing
between ancient iridescence
of dreamtime laughter

incandescent catacomb
of unrelenting fright

i sing you in this
world between words

ruminations i

(thoughts as you lay sleeping)

sometimes after slender petals of violet
sleep have lain themselves
across your face

i sit at the edge of everything
watching your tears
string into rosary

these are the times i travel you
without direction
or cartography

wishing you would
awaken   *mad diamond*
dancing me toward a brilliant sanity

i ache to tell you these things
but sometimes tongues
grow thick with words unspoken

and mouths clutter
with unuttered truths

but i listen
to that sadness hiding
in your mouth

like syllables of congealed pain

a song of clandestine salt
riding the back of sighing

and i am a book of psalms opening to you
daughter of desert
and dostoyevsky

death bringing mermaid
swimming in lament and sand

how have you come
to be the first and last
perennial of sunlight
chasing shadows from this land

how have i come
to run to you as horses
darkened by memory of sweat

fleeing memory of thirst

driven by an unknown knowing
of rivers ancient and giving
as the lines of your hands

how have i come to crave
the sanguine scent of wine
fermenting in the vat of your hips
surging to the urgings
of an outraged moon beckoning
i to pour my nights libation into you
and purge myself of self

and seek the consonants
of you

masking vowels
from blasphemous tongue
that your name remains
mantra chanted at the death of day

your name

a tetragrammic epiphany
of unjourneyed dreams

its existence
demanding i voyage
toward the primal
vowel

toward eternal seed
spinning at center
of creation

and find you
sleeping   *here*

in this beating church

this synagogue
of mass suicide

breathing
like this night
never to lift
from your cheek

like these words
you needed but
never coming
from my mouth

breathing
softly as your own
sorrow filled
silhouette

breathing
delicately
as the rituals of
unborn children

i will not know you

(for my friend teresa, a beautiful human being)

i have looked into your eyes
seen the butterflies
that wont take to the skies
because they fear the strength
in their wings

i have held your head in my lap
listened to you stigmata to the violent violin
of incessant grief

that night you cried
two of your tears
baptized my left palm

while you were not watching
i tasted them

swallowed them

began to know the taste
of the pain that drives

but i will not know you
until i have watched you sleep

no matter how many forevers
i dance with those strands
of gray in your hair
(lightning trapped
in the dark amber
of 2 a.m.)

no matter how many forevers
my fingers taste your feet
like slices of mango
slivers of a tangerine moon

or kiss your toes
hanging like grapes ripening
on vines of june

i will not know you
until i have watched you sleep
i will not know you

until i know
whether in hunger of
your slumber
your mouth still spreads
across your face

like peacocks plumage
when your lips labor
to give birth to
the hallelujah of your smile

or   if in sleep
do you   shiver frightened
of those demons you have been fighting
ever since you were that small defenseless child

i could spend infinities
licking laughter from
the teacup of your
navel

spend eternities
drinking secrets

from that wetness
which you weep

but these things mean nothing
not even shadowed substance

for i will not know you
until ive watched you sleep

i will not know you
until i have seen you there

lifting   drifting   floating
singing your cloud song
once you are cocooned
in communion
with the trinity of yourselves

seen you between
earth & sky

seen you between
ashe' & i

until i have seen you   peaceful   resting
as an angel   calm   accepting
tonight is the night
that she must die

i will not know you

until the strange knives of our bodies
have spooned themselves familiar

until i know the rhythm of star
pulsing in your chest

until ive seen your silver sheets of breath

weave themselves into papyrus
that your dreams inscribe upon

until ive seen your spirit
rise from flesh

run to meet your truest soulmate

then rush back into your body
as that first trumpet
of sunlight   daylight god-light

blares   blows   paints itself
a magenta jazz across the bosom of the skies

there is no need to penetrate you

i have already
spun universes
from the colors of your eyes

hykoo

viddles

you dance on i tongue
fillin me mouth wit yo song
like surps n cornbread

conja hans

conja hans voodoo a hoodoo
n d netherness uv mornin sheet

me rise   ignant ass yesternyt flame
a blak yookarist uv feer

i mouth   a premonition uv yeses
mutes 2 d kisscurve uv she sholder

hur b nokturnal sitar
canticalling homage 2 petrifyd star

an me r poet n wurd
unravellin tween lips
wut spell i illitrat

spellbound

when sun
slides high
in city skies
thighs come
cryin

from neath hems
of dresses wailing like hebrews
lost in asphalt wilderness

heavin cleavages
become hilled savannas
where giraffes and gazelles
laugh their spell
on our shit talkin transparencies

and men be come amethyst wind
in yo wake wantin to hug the stankin ankles
of women whose venomous asses
pass through us like *spiritus mundi*

we be come iambic sunlight
tongue-tied to the sweaty creases
hind knees fadin mirage like
into concrete distance

transmuted mute
by the sound of wet lips
smackin tween delicate legs
like epileptic kisses

our cool starts churchin
lord dont hurt me hymns
as you sanctify us
beneath the sweet swellin
arch of yo movement

and melt us

like fudgesickles
in the swelterin hell of yo hands

(a poem written to a woman who asked
why even the most articulate men having
street corner conversations shut up when women
walk by showing a thimble full of flesh in summer)

hykoo

mo˙viddles

can me wrap you up
take you home fur a late night snack
o maybe   breakfast

last lovin blues

on this night
our last   beloved

when we resurrect dead memory
and recall our faded dream

when our limbs stretch/caress
unreachable images

when our spines canter
arias of battered song
singeing us into metaphor

i will need to annihilate you

be meteor crushing world

become ash enveloping you
hide you from light
for unanswered millennia

this night i will beg you
to know
my blood

consume each haiku
written beneath this tongue
and name the countless children
ive bled to die on your thighs

this last night

i will echo the brown
ripple of your eyes
and walk
the wounded wind in your laughter:

timid/dark   an eritrean prayer
weeping from the wrists
of a dying poet

this last night

i am apostolate crawling through cathedrals of doubt
needing to retreat to the sanctity of your hands

dance deaf and deliberate
towards your dirges vibration

i need you this night to be
an indigo blues

simple
somber
filling me with pain

to remain
a trembling traveling death
inside me

moving in tempestuous fury

a storm stitched beneath my skin

lillie

i have deathed before
and will death again

in the god of your eyes

your tongue is mourning gallows
where i watch my self swing

i cannot traverse
this anorexic universe
of our separation
beating against the trees
of morning despair

my selves
weighted to
your powerful indifference

lillie

in your eyes all things visioning conjure

lillie

exhaled sigh of prophecy

a saxophone gasping beneath
nocturnal waters vomiting headless
angels swimming in quiet asphyxiation

how many maggoted moons
circle the center of your betrayal

how many rancid rings
be born in the silent saturn
of your smile

mira

mira   sugar spice
yellow/brown rice mama
con skin like caramel rivers
sun goddess knowing
the flowing of orbits
cycles/songs of sundial time

mira   ginger eyed queen
of everything
sable brown
raven hair gently
streaming down
your face like dark water fall
cascading into
fading into
blackness

look at me as i sigh
your name
dont cast your eyes
to earth in shame

aztec
soul sister
toltec
mind twister
weaver of beaded magic
see me as ive seen you

i was clothed and clouded
in shadow of olmec head
but i saw you

once i watched while you
stood naked on apex of pyramid

facing coming light
con feathers in your crown

once just once
i wish you would split
your lips

break the chain
binding that muscle of tongue
and speak to me

di me di me
speak to me

explain this urge to memorize
the mystery of your mouth

explain this urge to bend
the rigid straight of your body
to the curve of full moons
over ancient desert cities
and ride the mystical winged creature
of you into the blinding blazing glow
of starlight forevering your image in
amber constellation

explain this storm raging
in gentle fury beneath the sky of my skin
leaving your name in its wake

i want to know you

cinnamon umber
burnt orange rose petalled
rainbow

to be chocolate
smoke filled water
washing gently against
the supple beach of your thighs

carry grains of your sand
to shores of foreign lands
where men will erect altars
temples   synagogues
to the myth of you i will teach them
coax peyote
out of a bag full of your smiles

to be an ever present satellite
hanging on your cloak of night

when you look toward sky
i want you to see i
floating in blue/blackness
rotating revolving
in elliptical orbit
rhythmed round the
planet of your eminent becoming

hykoo

safiya boutta fall asleep

yo eyes r speakin
n hushed tones uf brown whisperz
callin 2 silence

in the year i loved your mother

(for my daughter safiya who needs to know this)

in the year i loved your mother
i lived a glorious death
i was satellite traveling between blood and star
a planet evolving through rage and grief

in the year i loved your mother
came the time of drought and deluge
a season of rain and ruin

between us   much soil and water
an illiterate ocean of language and diction

i arrived to her half broken half breaking

in the year i loved your mother
we were drum and drone
a volley of polemic and ideal

once   i glimpsed you
waving at me from her mouth
as dawn met our shoulders
she whispered me your name

we became the thin line
between sea and mountain
between valley and sky

in the year i loved your mother
gravity abandoned me to her
she was vortex - a black hole
sewn into the belly of a continent
crushing all into singularity

grapewaswinewas
soundwassongwas
motionwasdancewas
dovewasvulturecirclingwaslandingwas
all   that   was :   was   her

in the year i loved your mother
was the year of tragedy and tongue

we severed ours   stitched them into
one anothers mouths   we grew fluent in speaking pain

we brought stones from our pockets
traded them   hurled them back towards
each others wounds   and those that missed
were gathered later   were used to build our walls

your mother was an equinox of razors when i found her
an autumn of featherless wings
caught in this gale of a man

your mother was: soft lips cutting calluses
from my knuckles

a silk fist logged hard in my mouth
opening into a sunflower
widening in the crag of my throat

in her skin i was cryptic blasphemy
transparent   decoded   holy

Chants

rhythm

(9:50p.m. at velvet lounge chicago. 3/9/97)

struct ure

cen tered s om e where in the ha lo of skin

fe tal dis charge of all th ing s think ing/ flo at ing/
pass ing con scio us ness on/in 2 in fin it ies great/small

in tense mean ing wrapped
in 1 ness with so u nd of

tho ught s piercing through
o paque hor iz ons
of new days daw n ing in   w om b s   un formed

dig it

changeling

(for miles dewey davis)

an ill wind blew
that september
night you

turned into
a crow and flew

yo
solo
through

a storm of dust
and cloud

all
me could do

was watch

through the skull
of an entranced
voyeur

hung like
an embryo poem

on an olive branch

bird in labor with trane and sanders

hooooorns meltinnnnn
n2 hurrycaaaaaaiiins
molten lava torn at doze
swooooooooooooonin
swiiiiiiiiiiiiiiirlin n
maaaagma aingwish

sumthin
n me fights
2 b born

sumthin
n me struggoals 2
die e e ee e e ee

cant
stop it
stop it
stop it

cant
stop it
stop it
stop it

cant

2
much

fu fur fury

4 me

2
contain

there b

d mons
tryin 2

fu fu fuk
me brain

n

aingels
with jars uv k-y
stro kin up 4 d train

oya
blows soul
throo d mouth peace

bell
yells

sperm sails
re lease

n hellllll
follllowwwsss so so so

sumthin gotta go
sumthin gotta give
sumthin gotta die
sumthin gotta liiiivvve

horn melts

flames

curse
brass
2
brown
2
black
2
blacker
2
blackest

water bre bre breaks

makes
thunder
come

thunder
comes

thunder
cometh
like

br
e
a
th

breathe d thunder
push d wind
breathe d thunder

push d wind
breathe d thunder
push d wind

breathe d thunder

push d wind

breathe
thunder
push
wind
breathe
thunder
push
wind
breathe
thunder
push
wind
breathe
push
breathe
push
breathe
push
breathe
push
breathe
push   twins

hykoo

meelaz kissez

meelaz kissez fall
upon me face like rain drops
blessin d parched earth

dance jamila dance

I.

this night is alive

tongue
language
sound

alive

a tangled whisper
echoing around itself

II.

gods back
arches tward hell

gehenna flickers

from the bell

a serpents tongue
see   king   temperature

speak lord
speak to me

rhythm me the mystery
in the running of veins

dig on me
the wisdom
of yo spit

III.

my daughter
dances
beyond dance tonight

she is prayer
beyond ritual

ancestor say: black women move like this
when gods grab them

dance jamila
move jamila

teach me
all i refuse to remember

call the
old ones
down to
earth
ekua

jatizla

ramanah

jecumbnatah

let them initiate you

travel the path in your bones

bathe you in forgotten blood
screaming from oceans
and cotton fields

this
night is alive

something about
this night bleeds
when jamila dances

dance jamila dance

(written 5/18/97 at 7:50 p.m.
upon watching one of my daughters
dance to Mongo Santamarias "Afro Blue"
with Arthur Anderson on tenor sax)

jazz people

we sleep the dance of music
we walk the night of song
we be the bliss
hiding deep in the kiss
of a bass tone stretched out long

we breath the air in saxes
and relax on the backsides of suns
we be the rhythm
hidden deep inside the rhythm
we worship in the church
of drums

we be jazz people
living in ellas scats
and dizzies chants
from bulging cheeks
which speak and seek
to send us towards venus

we be red wind ripping
thru city streets gripping
like tigers teeth stripping
all flesh into shreds

weve been here
for a billion years
and few have ever seen us
we exist on a plane
where kisses rain

on you like snow in winter

weve abolished
the ignorant knowledge
of racial prejudice and gender

we dont understand
how it is that man
has a soul but refuses to use it

life is more fulfilling
when you are willing
to come and exist
in music

come   sleep the dance of music
come   walk the night of song
come   be the bliss
hidden deep in the kiss
of a bass tone stretched out long

come breath the air in saxes
come relax on the backsides of suns
come be the rhythm that slides
in the rhythm inside
of the church of drums

(a song derived out of improvisational
stories i tell my daughter jamila at bedtime)

51

hykoo

punk ass

unlike d song go
me b waaaayyy 2 proud 2 beg
oh pleez baby pleez!

hykoo

hint from da bakadabus

what would b d bomb
is while no 1 was watchin
yo mouth made i scream

(written to a girlfriend
on a bus ride back to chicago from detroit)

hykoo

jookin

gal yo hips b like
2 jook joints onna payday
an i'z ret ta dance

brotha to the night

(a blues for nina, the unabridged version)

ssssssssssoooooo

he no longer listens and you have finally come to me

why am i not surprised he listens to no one

you wish to know if there is still time
to rebel against him
still time to bring seed and sin
upon this heart of turquoise and cloud
time to escape this garden
of fastidious travel
these days of sad perfection
rotting in the mouth of longing

yes   i can show you how

i alone possess the powers
to the words of knowing

i watched you

i watched you watching the womb bathing in the river
beneath copper moon

she   a trembling night nipple gorged with blood
became question mark carved at the edge of your faith

and you felt something likening itself unto him
stir within you an unnamed unanswered vengeance

well i am the name and the vengeance

and i alone possess the words to the powers of knowing

i could bring her to you   you dig
could make her touch you in ways he could never imagine

he does not understand
the profane slap of skin

could make the two of you
bone of bone   flesh of flesh
sinew of sinew   breath of breath
make you handfuls of peeled grapes
clustering against one another
eternally exploding gently in naked profusion

i could do this for you i alone possess the words
of knowing

however   there is a price

from the union between
you and the womb
you will bear two seeds

you will give me   your first born you give him   your second
for once he will know how it is to come in behind me
to know what it means to stand in the shadow of denied light

will you do that for the words of knowing
will you do that to possess the womb

very well

tonight womb herself
sleeps in the clearing
beyond the trees

once moon

is closest to earth
and sons of the four winds
turn themselves toward
their cardinal directions

i will sing you to her   you will lay next to her
in the cool grass   and in her left ear
you will say   *thisssssssssssssssssssssssssssssssss*
sssssssssssssssssssssssssssssssssssssssss
sssssssay baby

can i be yo slave
ive got to admit girl
you the shit girl
i m diggin you
like a grave

come here you bundle of thistle laden pleasure

bet you taste like honey flavored pain
if i had a minute of yo time
to dig inside yo mind
i bet that i could play yo game

do they call you daughter to the spinning pulsar
or is it queen of ten thousand moons
baby sister to the distant yet rising star
is yo name yemaya or oshun

oooooo is that a smile me put on ya face chile
wide as a field of jasmine and clover
talk that talk honey walk that walk money
with them legs that could spank jeho——

ssshhhiiii

who am i

that aint important
but they call me brotha to the night

and right now
im the blues in yo left thigh
trying to become the funk in yo right

lets go some where and get   personal
see if you and i can crawl
inside a rip in the fabric of time
and ill sang you a psalm
of serpentine balm
while your lips sip the blackest wine

and ill be yo concubine

voodooful woman   santeria queen

yoruba princess of two headed magic
please dont ignore me when you hear me scream

i gots me a demon   that needs to be exorcised
i say i gots me a de de de de de de demon
thats in need of a little exercise

and i need you to come
speak in tongues
play yo drum

make my juju rissss
                    sss
                    sss
                    ssssssssssssssseesay baby
who am i

ill be whoever it is you say

but right now im the sightraped hunter
blindly pursuing you as my prey

and i want to slip you injections
of sublime erections   get you to dance
to my rhythm

make you scream archetypes
bout black angels in flight
on wings of distorted contorted   metaphoric jism

come on slim   fuck yo man
i ain t worried bout him

i gotta get you to step to my scene

cuz rather than deal with the phallicy
of this dried assed reality

id rather dance
yo sweet ass
in a wet dream

who am i

they call me brotha to the night

and right now
im the blues
in yo left thigh

trying to become
the funk in yo right

is that alriiiggghhhttt

funknawlegy

(a never ending quest)

"is there funk after death?   is seven up?"
                                    -parliament

!

funk

be the baby
of james browns loins
wet nursin corn liquor
from george clintons left nipple

a moon lipped lover
with moon shinin tongue
translatin the song
of footsteps heard sneakin
out back doors

funk

be a dance floor
filled with magenta faith
ridin ragin reefer smoke
into veins of a
brand new fix

funk

be the resurrected
scream of sunbeams
stumblin on junkies
noddin silently towards death

funk

be the honey suckle breath
of women made of star shit
comin in they lovers mouths
like holocausts of screams and laughter
opalescent banshees   shrouded in clouds
devoured in the snaggle toothed smile of night

!!

funk

be michael jacksons robot
turned funkadelic poplock

an epiphany brought by a thumb
thumpin strings of a fretless bass
buildin black sound thick enough to
stand on

so intangible
you cant put your hands on

funk

be a thousand fists risin
in rebellion and revolution
grabbin bits of sky
tryin to weave new solutions

funk

be rural blues
learnin to pimp in urban shoes
after payin city dues

warnin ! warnin !

good funk been known
to cause young girls
to find out theys gots hips to use

and this could turn
them into night mamas **(uuhh)**
with thighs **(uuhh)**
capable of punkin men **(good gawd)**
into pieces of dead religion

funk

be a head full of snappy naps
and cokabugs picked out
leanin like a halo
gleamin with the power
of afro sheen and disco baptism

funk

be the jism of a whisper
soothin as sage smoke
opiatin yo head in
twelve gauge thoughts

funk

be livin and dyin

be sighin and cryin

funk

be a sister swearin she gots
"good hair"

but the kitchen
don caught her ass lyin

funk

be a brand new hog
rollin in pretentious redness
down the center of
rainslicked ghetto streets

cuttin up asphalt
with all the tenacity
of a new car payment
through a welfare check

funk

be the groovy groove
of a lovers hand
dippin down to drown yo groin
in a project stairwell echoin the smelly serenade
of piss stains framed on gray walls like abstract hieroglyphs

funk

be somethin you got to go back
and get cuz

to dig what funk is
you gots to cop
what funk was

!!!

funk

was yo teeth stained green and red
from a combination of sour apple
and wala-melon nialters
and chic-o-stick breath
stankin to the tune of pop-rock candy

funk

by definition was not
jim nor dandy
amos nor andy
or barry man u low singing mandy

funk

was that three-quarter inch of embarrassin vaseline
black southern mamas rubbed on black
childrens faces on blustery winter mornins
fo we went off to school

cuz they
mississippi
alabama
tennessee
louisiana
georgia
arkansas
north
south cakalakee

common sense
told them that theoretically speakin
northern wind should whip round brown chillun faster
if we be properly lubricated

and funk was that feelin
of relief we felt upon
arrivin at school and diggin
how we was just one of a tiny   shiny
group of greasy faced youngsters

whose black southern mamas
was obviously matriculated
from the same school of thought

funk

was communion

funk

said come you on

funk

looked at you
like that last swig of red kool-aid
or piece of sweet potato pie
at a black family reunion

funk

was and is a sunday mornin
church girl singin first alto
in the choir
tryin to forget

all the sins she committed
on that saturday night funk found her

and funk was and is that brother
sittin way in the back
three hallelujahs
and a praise gawd
from the right who cant wait
til church is over so he can remind her

funk

be a **funkee** poet
knittin a **funkee** net
of **funkee** words

realizin the **funkee** futility
of tryin to capture **funk** in a poem

The Funkdamentals of Funknawledgy:

*Each generation has its own sound track: A music which "accompanies" the attitude and
prevailing drama of the times. The sound track of my generation was "funk". The times I
came up in were referred to as "when pimps and ho's slammed Cadillac doe's." It was the 70's
and America was using cocaine, heroin and free sex to try and assuage a potentially terminal
case of the viet-e.r.a.-civil-right-nam blues. African-American communities were hit hard. So
we partied to forget the pain of struggling. But it was, even in the madness, a wonderful time
to be alive.*

*Music, being an expression of the times in which it is born, is the recorded pulse of the
populace. We hear our own voice in the song. The song validates our living.*

it's a teenage thang

(for every teenager who has rebelled against their parents
by sneekin out to party)

bass slides in on all fours
rabid with feral look in eyes

bodies   twist
        into
     blasphemous
       angle of
   rebellion/defiance

somethin smellin
like   jail time

cuts across air
        like hand fulls of zirconia
scratchin shit
     out of plexiglass sky

over in corner
     cue balls psychotic   smack

breaks up tribe of stripes and solids
on field of green

               black eight sinks
           thru smoky haze of aw shits
         damns as ten spots reluctantly
             ruffle they ways
           out pissed off pockets

d.j. priest
sittin reverently in the pulpit
jacks sounds in alternatin patterns
of thirty three and thirds

spinnin gospel
of our faith
as congregations hands

reach heavenward
exposin our palm to angles

as we hope to catch a
hallowed high five
from a god whose
pissed cuz shes gotta work
the night shift

      tonight

we be young
virile   sweatin passions
ya gotta experience to understand

we dont give a damn
        bout tympanic
        cartilaginous erosion
        of inner ears

        weakened by 1200 to many
        hot grindin weekends
        of buttbumpinwoofinandtweetin

we dont give a damn
bout ass kickin
waitin on us when we get
home way past curfew

        (ok a little)

but tonight we only care bout
ass kickin bass and drum
can give

ass kickin bass and drum
can heal

tonight we live for strobelights
kissin vision and
bringin new sight

for floors moanin with
weight of young
flippant attitudes

glasses mumblin
speech of stolen
kisses

sky explodin with funk
of flirtin smiles

we live for bodega crew
comin up from barrio

bringin supple
brown morenas con
hips like congas
gon-boppin
6/8 rhythm
from front door to dance floor

got you tryin to speak in language
you aint never tongued before

uh   mira maimi   uh   pasie aqee po oon momentato po fayvo
(or somethin like that)

big   red   manzana lips
partin ever so slightly
revealin thin sliver of pink tongue
rollin like scarlet smoke off roof of latina mouths

                        we live for sisters
blue blacks   honey browns
            heavenly ebonies   gettin down
            on legs shaped like mamas soulfood
            with a whole lotta attitude

calves

        carved

            outta hams and hocks

with backsides big   round   sweet   and tender
as grandmamas homemade biscuits
(have mercy)

they hair icked
                slicked
                    tricked
                        or picked out
                            into
asymmetricalisoscelesrhomboidparallelograms

and a few other forms
defying geometric
classification

        tonight

we be young   virile
                    sweaty with passion
you gotta experience to understand

        tonight

be our night to hold somebodies body
to feel they eye lashes brush up against
face on slow jam

                    feel thin wispy fingers
                    of they breath invade
                    sensitive conch shell ear
                    like well trained guerillas

to hold them close   firm   heavin   nubile
against the mask of teenage knowin
and adolescent pretence

                    somethin deep inside us
                    that useta paint on caves
                    realizes this moment contains a forever
                    and eternal memories be born one forever at a time

        tonight

we be young   virile   sweaty with passions
you gotta

            understand to experience

and tonight we dont care or give a damn
why our parents dont seem to understand

that sweat   be a friend of ours
and tonight we gots to get real real
                                    friendly

It's a Teenage Thang:

My mother is a very devout Jehovah's Witness. and has been for most of my life. My father. at one time. was a Chicago police officer. Neither one of them would allow me or my brother Ron to go out and party. So my brother and I would sneak out of the home when mamma went to sleep and pops went to work.

We would take the C.T.A. (Chicago Transit Authority) east to Halsted Street or the Madison bus west to the "Factory" or the North Ave. to DaVinci Manor to get our groove on while listening to house music. Inside of those parties we found a new communion with others and ourselves. This is a late recollection of what it means to be young. defiant and feeling your oats at 16.

hykoo

voodoo chile

u came on snake wings
uf red turjid gitar licks
u left d same way

eulogy of jimi christ

"look at the sky
turn a hell fire red lawd
somebodies house is burnin down down down

look at the sky turn a hell fire red lawd
somebodies house is burin down down down down"......

-jimi hendrix

I.

burn it down

you burned it all the way down jimi

made us burn
in the flame
that became yo sound jimi

grabbed ol legba
by his neck
made him
show you yo respect

hoochieman
coochie man
stranglin him
hoochie coochie hoodooman
wrangled him voodoo chile

made
his
steel

strings sing
ache
bend
break

sin
capitulate
give in
to the will
of yo beautifully
blessed fingers

bewitchinly
bleedin
bittersweet
south paw
serendipitous
sighs

and strained
stratacaster tears

soothin burnin
twistin turnin
into steam
as they fell

no

careened
toward all hellbound souls

only to
roll

back into yo
gypsied eyes

to fornicate
copulate
be sodomized
by penetration beautiful
of sweatband born acid rain

II.

a purple haze runnin through
yo brain drained into the veins
of daytrippers turned acid angel
by yo gift of little wings

which with the aid
of yo mary cryin winds soared
not merely above
around and through
crosstown traffic

but along/well beyond
watchtowers to realm
where gods made love
to little miss strange
foxy ladies in little red houses
over yonder

and on rainy days
would sit back
shoot craps
with laughin sams dice
while boastin bout who had
the most experience

III.

how that musebruise
of yo sadomasochistic bluesoozed
through floors and l.s.d. doors

left psychedelic relics wrecked
on phosphorescent shores

talkin bout that night
you got right
at yo height

rocked woodstock
played yo remade
american anthem

had all the flowers
in the garden chantin

go head brotha
piss off the power
structure brotha

say fuck ya
to the structure brotha
one mo time one last time
befo its yo last time brotha

stick/move
hit/run
stick/move hit/run
try to get
yo ass beyond
the grip of the grim one

try to get
yo ass out of
the sight line of death

try to get
yo ass past
the reach
the reaper

by dodgin
that sonofabitch
betwixt the expanse
of jangled cacophonous chords
and hidin out in shadows flooded with feedback
jimi the anointed
jimi the christ

jimi

you manically depressed
maniacally duressed
manifested messiah

impaled upon the neck
of that thang you loved the best
yo one hearts true burnin desire

jimi christ

forever walkin
on the waters
of a bad trip

turnin all of
them bad trips
into wine

castin yo net
upon the waters
of a bad trip
just to see whats there
for you to find

jimi   christ
patron saint
of divine distortion

too soon
did you force
the hand of demise

but i aint pissed
gypsy eyes

cause right now
we diggin on the thought
of you and yo homeboy god

bein somewhere
out there in electric lady land
sippin celestial moonshine

bout to tune axes
cut heads
and go
toe to toe
blow for blow
lick for lick
stick for stick

jimi   christ

too soon did you force
the hand of demise

but i aint pissed
gypsy eyes

cause i dig that any mother lover
who lived a life like you lived
deserved to die any death desired

to die youngto die
highto die stonedto
die freeto die youngto die high

to die stonedto die
freeeeeeeeeeeeeeeeeeeeee

all we wanted was one time
just   one   time

to   stand   next   to yo fire

the word

( )

an ochre song called you
from the corners of post existence

you appeared a silent apparition
of language

i became pregnant with the *word*

the word

took flight
on crimson oceans of light

oceans of light

screamed prayer
into vermilion angles
of wrangled space

wrangled space

sank like an obsidian siren
into the mad mouth of my pocket

my pocket

dangled a jangling death
from the tongue of a stone victrola

a stone victrola

coughed a murder of crows
shrieking translucent blue music

blue music

circled the bells
of my waiting
and insistent speech

my speech

oracled itself
toward the sword
of your memory

your memory

casted the shadow
of my castrated breath

my breath

cried the kiss
of an ochre song

calling you from the corner
of post existence

you appeared
a silent apparition of language

i became pregnant with the word

(( ))

the word

was born

was born   still

was stillborn
in center of turbulent
awakening
became sunlight carving her arpeggio
into archipelago of flat unfolding blackness

the word became

became shards of dead stars
shedding the egg of plant and planet

became constellated tongue
of demon and deity
lamenting the birth
of its form

became misspelled literature of tree
floating through abysmal
womb of the i

became
primordial hymn
sang from ancient azure stone

((( )))

i saw   word

saw   word   knocked up
knocked up sn or t ing her de ath
in sy lla bles

drinking her liver
in dilapidated taverns
on deathdwelt corners
without name

her fingertips ripped
cracked and bleeding raw
from clawing the insides
of forty ounce coffins

severed the leg of the x
manifested as man
riddled forty one times
by mystery of lead

left to die   floating
face up   eyes open
memory bleeding from hole in head

back to the i

word became

became broken vowel
hungry howling dying child
dragged to death

decapitated

sodomized by wood

was beaten mercilessly
for loving the loins of other men

the word was resurrected after three days
from the muddied river bottoms of a nations
bloody conscience

word inverted self
womanifested as violated
female flesh
slicked with slime
of patriarchy

word was entered by her father
so many times she learned to
believe his sickness
was sacred

(((( ))))

i loved word

danced with word
seven insistent salsas
till three a.m.

word was not afraid
to throw her head back
her arms skyward

and in white flashes of teeth
and sweat licked hair
mouth incomprehensible mumbling

timed to the rumblings
of unsounded sound

word sucked my tongue
as i dreamt this

word spit hibiscus balm
into my mouth

word and i
loved that night

i came into

untocriedanddiedinside
word
that
night

and word
became pregnant with
word
grew inside
word
gave birth to
word

word became
a brown childs fingers
wiping tears from
her fathers eyes

word became

word became
brown childs kisses
blooming in spite

of the hurricane

word became

word reached

to embrace brown thin
wrinkled hands
of brown thin wrinkled woman
who stirs pots of five a.m. grits
in cornerstone called mississippi

word lives
inside the universal shit thin
spaces of in/exhalation

traverses earth
trapped in condominiums of skin

forgetting and refusing to remember
she is I AAAAAMMMMMMMMMMM

The Word:

This is undoubtedly one of the most disturbing poems for me to read in public. I don't feel that I have ever read it properly. The images have been collected over a period of about ten years. The first part of the poem is replete with objects I find in my subconscious whenever I dream about June (my first girlfriend who died in a fire) or about my father Woody (who died of a heart attack).

The next part of the poem is a personal exploration of where I believe my words and images come from. This is a poem I don't understand yet. And the truth is, I was reluctant to publish it. Maybe I will get to understand it more now that it's in your hands

canticles and curses

(love letters found on a vagabond muse)

eyes

unclothed

you are unconquerable
a smile   slanted   curved
moonlight traveling your face
determined as an ounce of storm

laughing

you are green as southern summer
cotton and clay in your eyes
an arm flung vast and welcoming
an outstretched hand
an open palm

sleeping

you are small as your mouth
round   alive with scent of
slumbering earth

you are there and un-there
a mask of faces
sculpture and un-sculpted stone
a veiled visage of forethought
stretched between forms:

the diurnal finger which
touches me beneath my eyelids

mind

dark intellect   un-illumned demon
faltering abandon of slanted noon
we found one another surrounded by bodies
near the clarity of civilized deserts

overhead   obfuscated circles told of
vultures searching

we invoked this gehenna
where mercenary nightmares
tunneled through our sanctity

and indecision more certain
than the fugue of mallets

marched toward our shared space

where fear shattering our balance
became hobbled foot beneath
our stumbling love

blood

i remember you as woman river
or apsara with flaming sword
your body a pure sun stroked coral
your womb a hollering space of god-song

you were slow metaphor
lazily turning in my
tissue

a nocturnal shepherd
guiding word from my mouth
through arias of slim crimson rhythm

breath

angling in slivers of i
the wind thins your scent of albumen
your musk   masking nights
with a thousand hymns becoming

melisma   growing beyond
the lines of nation and nebula

we set flame to our sex that life
poured ourselves again into the body
of the dreamer :we: insomniac seeds
awaiting our hour of sleep and breath

belief

reborn

i became a faithless city
a dark dirge of alleys
frigid with incandescence

a transient alphabet ignorant of
octave and syllable

when came this shadow of shards
this cadenza of derelict shrapnel shaped of words:

poetry

her laughter   hungry and ferocious
her teeth of eyes scavenging my youth

her symphony of empty lots and street lamps
splintering my hearing into song

pilgrim

an inebriated spring prophesied
your return would gather us
                in breeze

me remained

solid as baobob poplar oak

even when urge came
to uproot   ride wild wind

now   siring leaf and fruit
            i hear you calling

            a siren song-ing

autumn
trapped in your teeth

thirst

when i tire of singing this
idiocy of testicles
i pray for the sun
you keep in your mouth

i call you   gatherer of light
who resting your hand on my side
leaves benediction in this space
of missing rib

you answer in canticle and curse

my throat strips raw with your coming
my lips crack in your absence

obeisance

i dreamed you were reciting my dream
i am urge pressed against air
pleading against ear

you are tongue conducting
me into language

i am black song:
an arrogant movement
tamed by your savage mouth

blooz man

I. unspoken knowin

god is a blooz man

sittin cross legged
with an axe angled
out his lap

lovin and revilin us all
like flatted thirds
presses gainst
frets of pain

god is a blooz man

what got life and death
strung like strings
cross his lovers neck

hear him prowlin
round alleys
of our minds
tryin to find
children cryin
from fear of night

now   god

believin its his man given right
to ambush any bodies head
whose coppin thoughts bout him

ambushed mine

one time takin
shape of a ghost note
cooin fugues of rain out the mouth

a mouth transformed into
a dimly lit window

placed eastward in backwater
shack of sky

window i creeped to
peeped through
dug myself as vishnu
sleepin on beds of lotus

dreamtimin bout creation and crossroas
etched in my hands

and at that cross in the road
where consciousness shatters
vision to awaken demand

at cross in the road
came man i would be
my humanity
began to expand

now i understand

i is the blooz man
the blooz man is i

II. realization

i is whine of all things terrible
the scream of all things tremblin

seraph whose wings beat hatred
the demon who smiles redemption

i is whisper cushionin
broken bodies in this sepulcher
of tumultuous existence

i is the blooz man
the blooz man is i

i is blushin flesh of quiverin virgin
i is ho who blows dawns

i is throbbin eye of battered wife
wonderin where her husbands gone

i is song of fatherless generations
sired by loins of war

i is comin of bedouin soldier
bringin smashin to heads and culture

i is white sail blown by winds of profit
salin on seas of severed black hands

i is the blooz man
the blooz man is i

i is ornament forged from all shackled human freedoms
an eagles feather trampled neath hooves of final solution

i is shamed thighs of all raped women
demandin the rapists death as retribution

blooz man

99

a black boot steppin
goose steppin/stompin
down the doors of scapegoats

blooz man

screamin stream of ash
blackenin skies over bergen-belsen
dachau and auschwitz

blooz man

i is cuttin edge
of rusted blades

and mouth
of gapin wound

the angry innocence
of questionin blood
demandin to be answered soon

baptism inside exorcism

missin eye of collective myopia

elegy of praise buried within
fecundity of all anathema

i is fingers of dead lovers still ticklin one another
cross mine fields
of war torn lands

i is the blooz man
the blooz man is i

III. acceptance

bring me tears
of a five year old son
wonderin if he ll
ever fill his daddies shoes at all

and i ll give you
soft eyed grin of a father
knowin one day those shoes
will grow too small

bring me choir of homesong
sang in exile as your feet trod sod
of stranger

and i ll show you star to guide you toward your own miracu-
lous births in manger

i is knockin
i is door

i is that voice both harsh and warm

that last bit of will
your pain cannot kill

a fine thread of sun
in lifes tapestry of storms

listen to jangle
and discord of my
sonata and hear

within its pale blue murmurrin
a thin cry of hope

listen to single flower
sighin while fightin its way
through cracks of concrete

and hear i split wind
and cheat death with breath
of human survival

i is the blooz man
the blooz man is i